The Lost Temple
of the Maya

Rob Waring, *Series Editor*

HEINLE
CENGAGE Learning

Australia • Brazil • Japan • Korea • Mexico • Singapore • Spain • United Kingdom • United States

Words to Know

This story is set in Guatemala [gwɑtəmɑlə], a country in Central America. It happens in a place where there was a city called El Mirador [ɛl mɪrədɔr] long, long ago.

 The Maya Civilization. Read the paragraph and look at the picture. Then match each word with the correct definition.

During the Classic Period from around 250 A.D. to 900 A.D., the ancient Maya civilization was one of the greatest groups of people in the world. They built cities with thousands of buildings including pyramids for kings, and huts where poorer people lived. These pyramids were also used as temples where Maya people went to show respect to their gods. They were also places to bury the dead. After their deaths, Maya kings were usually placed in tombs within these pyramids.

1. civilization _____	**a.** a small, simple building often made of wood
2. pyramid _____	**b.** place a dead body underground
3. hut _____	**c.** a building where people go to pray to a god
4. temple _____	**d.** the culture and society of a people
5. bury _____	**e.** a special place where a dead person is put
6. tomb _____	**f.** a building with a square base and four triangular sides

a pyramid

An Ancient Maya City

a tomb

a hut

B Digging into the Past. Read the paragraph. Then complete the definitions.

Archaeologists are scientists who study the past to discover new things about history. They often dig into the earth to find the ruins of ancient cultures. This story is about archaeologist Richard Hansen. Hansen is very interested in the pyramids of El Mirador which have been lost under the thick jungles of Guatemala. He thinks that the pyramids can tell him more about the Preclassic Period of the Maya.

1. The remains of very old buildings are also known as r_____.

2. To break up and move soil is to d_____.

3. A tropical forest in which trees and plants grow close together is a j_____.

4. A person who studies buildings, objects, and culture of ancient people is an a_____.

An Archaeologist Digging in Ruins

Preclassic	Classic	Postclassic
2,000 B.C. 250 A.D.	900 A.D.	1,500 A.D.

B.C. = time period before the birth of Jesus Christ*
A.D. = time period after the birth of Jesus Christ*
* in Christian calendar

Approximate Time Periods of the Maya

Archaeologists have been researching the Maya civilization for a long time. Now, in the middle of the Central American country of Guatemala, archaeologists are finding new **evidence**[1] about the ancient Maya. They're discovering a Maya world that may have existed long before scientists thought it did. The secrets of this new discovery may lie under the leaves and dirt of the Guatemalan jungle. They could be in or near one of the biggest pyramids ever built: the great pyramid of Danta.

Archaeologist Richard Hansen has traveled to the site of the pyramid. He suspects that the area around it, which is called the Mirador, may hold important **clues**.[2] By studying these clues, he may find information about the origins of one of the world's greatest civilizations. He thinks that they may unlock the secrets of the early Maya.

---

[1]**evidence:** words or objects that support the truth
[2]**clue:** a sign or information that helps fix a problem or answer a question

 CD 1, Track 07

The culture that is thought of as the 'Classic Maya' grew across Central America between 250 A.D. and 900 A.D. However, archaeologists are now discovering a Maya civilization that existed 1,000 years before the Classic Period. The Maya may have been a successful culture as early as the time referred to as the Preclassic Period. Most of the remains of this newly discovered culture lie under the earth in the Mirador region. They can be found near an ancient city that has been lost for hundreds of years: El Mirador.

Hansen has worked for more than 20 years at the lost city of El Mirador. During that time, he has been trying to understand the mystery of the early Maya. There are many questions to be answered. Who were they? How did they achieve so much? Hansen hopes to find the answers by digging under the pyramids. He hopes to find the tombs of the ancient kings of the early Maya.

Fact Check: True or false?

1. The Maya civilization is over 1,000 years old.

2. The Preclassic Period comes after the Classic Maya Period.

3. The ruins of El Mirador are in the jungle.

4. Richard Hansen has been working in Guatemala for 30 years.

As Hansen explores the area around El Mirador, he decides to climb Danta. He talks about the huge pyramid as he climbs it. "Well, this is the third level of the great pyramid of Danta at El Mirador, the largest pyramid at the site. It **sustains**[3] for nearly half a mile on **platforms**[4] below us here, and [it's] probably one of the largest pyramids in the world."

The Danta pyramid was built during a time period that many people consider to be basic and simple. But if the early Maya were so simple, how did they build a structure that is as complex as the Great Pyramids of Egypt?

---

[3]**sustain:** *(unusual use)* go on; continue for a distance or period of time
[4]**platform:** a flat, raised structure

Danta Pyramid

platform

.5 miles = 805 meters

El Mirador

The great pyramid of Danta at El Mirador is the largest pyramid at the archaeological site.

According to Hansen, things during the time period of the early Maya were not as simple as scientists once thought. He says that the kings of the early Maya civilization were as important as the kings of the ancient Egyptian civilization. "The person that **commissioned**[5] this building was not a simple chief, living in a grass hut," he explains, "This was a king on the order of **Ramses and Cheops**."[6]

---

[5]**commission:** arrange for someone to do a piece of work
[6]**Ramses and Cheops:** [ræmsiz] [kiɒps] two powerful ancient Egyptian kings

Infer Meaning

1. How does Hansen feel about the Maya kings?

2. What does the phrase 'on the order of' mean?

Some early Maya kings were as powerful as the ancient Egyptian kings.

Hansen dreams of finding these kings from the beginning of the Maya civilization. He hopes that their tombs will show who they were. He's especially excited to find out more about them as individuals. Most archaeological discoveries focus on the physical evidence, or outer signs, of the power and influence of the kings. Hansen says that there's not a lot of knowledge about them as people. Hansen feels that the work that archaeologists are doing in Mirador may help scientists get to know the kings more personally. What were they like and how did they live? Their tombs in the pyramids may unlock these clues.

Stone from El Mirador Temple

Hansen is especially interested in one of the smaller pyramids of El Mirador. One of the stones in the pyramid has a large **jaguar paw**[7] with three **claws**[8] on it. Hansen believes that this could be the tomb of an important Maya king who ruled from 152 B.C. to 145 B.C. during the Preclassic Period. The king's name means 'Great Fiery Jaguar Paw.'

As Hansen examines the stones of the pyramid, he talks about the discovery. "This may be a **symbol**[9] of [the king]," says Hansen, "that's why this building is so interesting to us, because it's possible this king could be buried here."

----

[7]**jaguar paw:** the foot of a large, wild cat that lives in Central and South America
[8]**claw:** the sharp nails on the feet of some animals
[9]**symbol:** sign or object that is used to represent something

jaguar

paw

claw

Is the 'Jaguar Paw' king buried in the temple? Hansen wants to find out. He has brought in a mapping expert and the newest technology in underground imaging systems. This special equipment sends electrical currents through the ground. These currents determine whether the ground is solid, or if there is an opening under it. The system then uses this information to create an image, or map, of what is under the soil. This map will show any open spaces in the parts of the pyramid that are underground. Will the imaging system show an empty room? If it does, this might be a place where Hansen could find the king's tomb. Hansen is very excited to get started!

The mapping expert prepares all of his equipment and sets up his computer. He then starts using the information from the equipment to create the map. After three hours, he calls Hansen over to his computer screen. He has a result. The system expert explains that there is an open space under the pyramid. The room, or chamber, is about 11 meters[*] under the earth. It's approximately eight meters long by two meters wide. That's just the right size for a king's tomb!

Hansen may soon make a major archaeological discovery. They may have found the tomb of an early Maya king. How does he feel about it? "It's exciting. Yeah, this is exciting," he says with a big smile.

_____

[*]See page 32 for a metric conversion chart

Hansen's team begins to dig. He is determined to prove that 'Great Fiery Jaguar Paw' really existed all those years ago. The digging continues for some time. It's a challenging project as there's a lot of rock and dirt to move. Hansen gives a report on their progress. "We've gotten about 13.5 **yards**[10] into the building now," he says, "and that represents about 22 **cubic yards**[11] of rock that we've brought out of there."

Hansen and his team dig deep into the Jaguar temple. Finally, they arrive at the place where the equipment showed a space—the room that might be the king's tomb. The team could be just a few minutes away from finding the tomb of the 'Great Fiery Jaguar Paw.' The team digs a short distance further. Then, they begin to pull away the last stones in front of the place where the opening is supposed to be. Everyone is very excited …

---

[10]**yard:** 1 yard = 0.91 meters
[11]**cubic yard:** measurement showing volume; a space that is 1 yard wide, 1 yard long, and 1 yard tall

… but there is disappointment waiting on the other side of the wall. The room is not the tomb of the king. There is nothing behind the chamber wall when they break through. Hansen explains, "There should have been a chamber or something there on the other side of this wall."

How does Hansen feel about the unexpected result? "This is a **setback**,"[12] he says unhappily, "There should have been something there." Hansen isn't completely disappointed though. He manages to come to a lighter conclusion about the kings who are so amazingly difficult to find. "So, the fact that it's not there," he says, "tells us that the **elusive**[13] **Kan kings**[14] are still elusive."

---

[12]**setback:** a problem that stops or undoes progress; a disappointment
[13]**elusive:** difficult to find
[14]**Kan kings:** [kɑn kɪŋz] a series of Maya kings from around 1000 B.C. to 300 A.D.

Summarize

Imagine that you are a TV or newspaper reporter. Make a short report about the search for the tomb of 'Great Fiery Jaguar Paw'. Tell a partner about it or write about it in your notebook.

Does this mean that the mystery of the early Maya kings is just a story after all? Hansen doesn't think so. He still feels that they are real and he's not content to give up easily. The lost tombs are difficult to find, but that doesn't mean that they don't exist. Hansen is preparing to dig at another pyramid next year. Perhaps then this archaeologist will achieve his goal of seeing the tomb of an early Maya king. Maybe he will finally find what he is looking for in the lost temples of the Maya.

After You Read

1. Archaeologists found a big pyramid _____ a jungle in Guatemala.
   A. below
   B. to
   C. on
   D. above

2. In paragraph 2 on page 4, the word 'hold' can be replaced by:
   A. contain
   B. show
   C. create
   D. cover

3. Which of the following is an appropriate heading for page 6?
   A. Maya Civilization Is 1,000 Years Old
   B. Preclassic Period Comes After Classic
   C. Ancient Maya Society Found
   D. Archaeologists Discover Modern Maya Period

4. Hansen thinks that the Danta pyramid shows that the early Maya:
   A. enjoyed the jungle
   B. built a basic pyramid
   C. were not simple
   D. were basic

5. On page 12, who is 'he'?
   A. Ramses
   B. Hansen
   C. the Maya chief
   D. an Egyptian leader

6. The jaguar paw symbol is very interesting to Hansen because:
   A. The pyramid might be the tomb of a famous king.
   B. He can use special equipment to dig up earth.
   C. The stones show there is a room inside.
   D. A claw means there is an empty space below.

7. The special equipment can help discover _____ is inside the pyramid.
  A. that
  B. how
  C. what
  D. where

8. On page 18, 'it' in the phrase 'If it does' refers to the:
  A. imaging system
  B. king
  C. space
  D. map expert

9. In paragraph 1 on page 21, 'a result' can be replaced by:
  A. some news
  B. a decision
  C. a solution
  D. an idea

10. Which of the following is NOT a good heading for page 25?
  A. Preclassic King Is Still Unknown
  B. Elusive Jaguar Paw Tomb Discovered
  C. Setback Disappoints Archaeologist
  D. No Room on Other Side of Wall

11. What is still part of the mystery of the Kan kings?
  A. where their tombs are
  B. who the kings were as people
  C. if the kings existed or not
  D. all of the above

12. What is the main purpose of the story?
  A. to show that the Kan kings probably didn't exist
  B. to explain why pyramids were built
  C. to show one man's search for answers about the early Maya
  D. to explain the difference between ancient Egyptian kings and Maya kings

The Maya View of the World

Much of the information that we have about the Maya was found in Maya ruins. The temples and pyramids that were built by ancient Maya kings are an important resource for scientists. By using information discovered in Mexican and Central American jungles, archaeologists have learned a great deal about Maya history and everyday life. They have discovered many interesting aspects of Maya culture which can tell us more about them.

The Maya people had an unusual and advanced numbering system. At the time, most of the world had no concept of the number zero. The Maya, however, were using a flat, round shape as a symbol to represent this amount. Their counting system had only three symbols: a dot, which represented one, a bar for five, and the round shape for zero. Certain numbers were considered extremely important by the Maya. For example, 20 was special because it equaled the number of fingers and toes that could be used for counting. The number 52 represented the number of years in a Maya century.

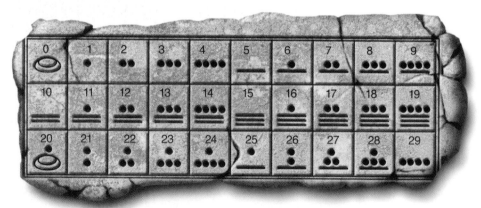

The Maya Numbering System

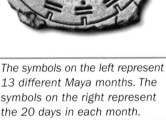

The symbols on the left represent 13 different Maya months. The symbols on the right represent the 20 days in each month.

The Maya calendar offers another surprising look at how they organized information differently from other cultures. They didn't use a chart with rows of numbers representing days and months. They used several different circular calendars at the same time. One calendar contained 13 months consisting of 20 days each for a total of 260 days. This calendar was used for religious purposes and for planting their fields. Another calendar had 365 days and was based on the movement of the planets. When the Maya referred to both calendars, they matched their twenty-day months with the 365-days in the planetary calendar. When they did this, the days that were left over at the end of the year were considered very unlucky.

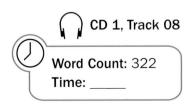

CD 1, Track 08

Word Count: 322
Time: _____

Vocabulary List

archaeologist (3, 4, 6, 15, 21, 26)
bury (2, 17, 18)
civilization (2, 4, 6, 9, 12, 15)
Classic Period (2, 3, 6, 9)
claw (17)
clue (4, 15)
commission (12)
cubic yard (22)
dig (3, 9, 22, 26)
elusive (25)
evidence (4, 15)
hut (2, 12)
jaguar paw (17, 18, 22)
jungle (3, 4, 9)
platform (10, 11)
Preclassic Period (3, 6, 9, 17)
pyramid (2, 3, 4, 9, 10, 11, 15, 17, 18, 21, 26)
ruins (3, 9)
setback (25)
sustain (10)
symbol (17)
temple (2, 16, 18, 22, 26)
tomb (2, 9, 15, 17, 18, 21, 22, 25, 26)
yard (22)

Metric Conversion Chart

Area
1 hectare = 2.471 acres

Length
1 centimeter = .394 inches
1 meter = 1.094 yards
1 kilometer = .621 miles

Temperature
0° Celsius = 32° Fahrenheit

Volume
1 liter = 1.057 quarts

Weight
1 gram = .035 ounces
1 kilogram = 2.2 pounds